Punctuation Manual

Published

By

Edson Mazira

ISBN 978-0-7974-8363-7

Punctuation Manual

© Edson Mazira, 2020

CONTENTS

INTRODUCTION

Punctuation Manual provides with basic lessons on how and where to use commas, semicolons, colons, en dashes, em dashes, ellipses, periods, exclamation marks, question marks and other punctuation marks.

According to the *Concise Oxford Dictionary— Tenth Edition*, punctuation is defined as *the marks, such as full stop, comma, and brackets, used in writing to separate sentences and their elements and to clarify meaning.*

Punctuation marks are for everyone regardless of school levels.

THE USE OF A COMMA

The comma (,) is misused in many cases. Although it's popularly known that the comma is used where you want to pause, there are certain rules of using it. You don't just use it anywhere you think or feel you have to use it.

Commas may appear to be too many in a written piece, but each of them has its specific role.

When the comma is used incorrectly, it alters the whole meaning of a sentence. You need to be very careful about where and how to use it.

Study the following lessons on the use of a comma:

Lesson 1

Separating dependent sentences from independent sentences

A comma is used to separate a dependent clause from an independent clause:

1. *If James sees Mary*, he will be happy.
2. *Although Pfumvu is poor*, he is always cheerful.
3. *When you go*, don't forget to carry this.
4. *Since you are one of them*, you can take it.

Lesson 2

Separating non-restrictive relative clauses and non-restrictive appositive nouns from main clauses

Commas separate non-restrictive relative clauses or non-restrictive appositive nouns or noun phrases from main clauses.

Examples of relative clauses:

    a. who donated these books
    b. whom I talked to
    c. which she bought

Look at how the commas work in this:

1. Edson, *who donated these books*, is a writer.
2. I gave it to Mike, *who forwarded it to Tracy*.

When the non-restrictive relative clause is in the middle of a sentence, don't forget to use two commas (the first comma and the second comma):

1. Knowledge, *whose brother bought a new car yesterday* wants to help us. [Wrong]

Always remember to use the second comma:

2. Knowledge, *whose brother bought a new car yesterday*, wants to help us. [Correct]

Appositive nouns or noun phrases, those nouns or noun phrases that follow after and rename or identify other nouns or noun phrases, are separated with commas when they are nonrestrictive. They are treated the same as the non-restrictive relative clauses.

Examples:

1. Edson Mazira also, *one of the Zimbabwean authors*, is visiting us. [Correct]
2. Edson Mazira also, *one of the Zimbabwean authors* is visiting us. [Wrong]
3. I saw Edson Mazira, *one of the Zimbabwean authors*.

Number 2 is wrong because the second comma, after the appositive noun phrase, is missing.

Another mistake is of using a comma between the subject (of a sentence) and the predicate (the finite verb with its entire modifiers):

1. *My dog and his cat*, are not friends. [Wrong]
2. *My dog and his cat* are not friends. [Correct]

Note:

- Use both commas for a non-restrictive relative clause when it is in the middle of a sentence.

- Use both commas for a non-restrictive appositive noun or noun phrase when it is in the middle of a sentence.
- Never use a comma to separate the subject from its predicate.

Lesson 3

Separating nouns of address and interjections from main clauses

Commas separate nouns of address from main clauses. A noun of address is that noun mentioned or called—in a direct speech—to draw someone's attention.

Examples:

1. *Edson*, follow me.
2. Follow me, *Edson*.
3. Do you know, *Edson*, that I'm a soldier?

Don't forget to use both commas when the noun of address is in the middle of a sentence:

1. Do you know, *Edson* that I'm a soldier? [Wrong]
2. Do you know *Edson*, that I'm a soldier? [Wrong]

It's also wrong to entirely leave out the commas:

3. *Edson* follow me.
4. Follow me *Edson*.
5. Do you know *Edson* that I'm a soldier?

Using commas to treat interjections

An interjection is a word or a group of words used to express feelings and so on.

Examples of interjections:

1. Hi
2. Umm
3. Wow
4. Eh
5. mm

The interjection—apart from being treated with a period, an exclamation mark, and so on—is treated with commas.

Examples:

1. *Umm*, I've no idea.
2. I've, *mm*, two points.

When the interjection is in the middle of a sentence, use both commas.

Lesson 4

Separating absolute phrases from independent sentences

Commas separate absolute phrases from independent sentences:

1. The old man waited for the bus, *a big hat on his head.*

2. *A big hat on his head,* the old man waited for the bus.
3. The old man, *a big hat on his head,* waited for the bus.

Don't forget to use both commas when the absolute phrase is in the middle of a sentence:

1. The old man, *a big hat on his head* waited for the bus. [Wrong]
2. The old man *a big hat on his head,* waited for the bus. [Wrong]

Lesson 5

Coordinating conjunctions and independent sentences

Coordinating conjunctions are conjunctions used to join phrases or sentences. They've FAN BOYS as their acronym, which stands for *for, and, nor, but, or, yet* and *so.* When the coordinating conjunction joins two independent sentences, a comma precedes it. This is very common with long sentences; when the sentences are short, the use of the comma is optional.

Examples:

1. The hunter fired several bullets at the animals, *and* they all ran away.
2. The hunter fired several bullets to the animals, *but* he killed none.

Don't place the comma after the coordinating conjunction:

1. The hunter fired several bullets at the animals *and,* they all ran away. [Wrong]
2. The hunter fired several bullets to the animals *but,* he killed none. [Wrong]

Lesson 6

The serial / Oxford comma

Commas are used in a list of elements. The last element, before we write 'and', is either given a comma or not. This comma is called the serial comma or the Oxford comma.

Examples:

1. I saw a lion, an elephant, a leopard and a zebra.
2. I saw a lion, an elephant, a leopard, and a zebra.

The comma after leopard is the serial comma or the Oxford comma.

The choice on using the serial comma mainly depends on whether you're using the US English or the UK English.

Lesson 7

Interrupters

Commas are used to separate interrupters from main clauses. An interrupter is a word or a group of words that comes in the middle of a sentence.

Examples:

1. James, *I'm sure*, is a soldier.
2. James, *according to the reports I got from those boys yesterday*, is a soldier.

Don't forget to use both commas:

1. James, *according to the reports I got from those boys yesterday* is a soldier. [Wrong]
2. James *according to the reports I got from those boys yesterday*, is a soldier. [Wrong]

Lesson 8

Separating modifiers

We use a comma to separate a subject modifier when it comes after the object of the sentence or after an intransitive verb (without the object). Do you understand this? By saying a subject modifier, I mean a word or phrase that modifies the subject. The subject is the agent of the action in a grammatical sentence. The object is the sufferer of the action. However, the lesson is not about the subject and the object; it's about using the comma to separate the modifier that comes at the end.

Examples:

1. "Where?" he asked, *confused.*

'Confused' is modifying the subject 'he' *that he was confused.* If we remove the comma, 'confused' modifies 'asked', which is wrong for such an adjective to modify a verb.

2. "Where?" he asked *confusedly.*

'Confusedly' is modifying 'asked', the verb. If we use a comma after 'asked', 'confusedly' modifies 'he', which is wrong for such an adverb to modify a pronoun.

Note:

1. "Where?" he asked, *confused.* [Correct]
   "Where?" he asked *confused.* [Wrong]

2. "Where?" he asked *confusedly.* [Correct]
   "Where?" he asked, *confusedly.* [Wrong]

Lesson 9

Direct speech

Don't use a comma at the end of a direct speech if you have used a question mark or an exclamation mark to end the direct speech.

Examples:

1. "Where?," he asked. [Wrong]
2. "Hey!," she exclaimed. [Wrong]

When the comma is required, don't forget to use it:

1. "I know him" she said. [Wrong]
   She said "I know him." [Wrong]

Lesson 10

Phrases or clauses working as subjects

Never use a comma to separate a phrase or clause that is working as the subject of a sentence.

Examples:

1. *Talking to John,* is what I'll do next. [Wrong]
   Talking to John is what I'll do next. [Correct]

2. *Today,* is a good day for me. [Wrong]
   Today is a good day for me. [Correct]

3. *That Godfrey was one of the robbers,* shocked me. [Wrong]
   That Godfrey was one of the robbers shocked me. [Correct]

Lesson 11

Separating introductory phrases

Commas separate introductory phrases from main clauses.

Examples:

1. *Here and there,* Nhamo lifted up her new shoes to check their soles.
2. *On the table,* Tinashe spread out his map.
3. *Outside the building,* there were people shouting.

These commas are optional when the phrases are too short. Peter Herring, one of the grammarians in the world, wrote that the comma is optional when the phrase is less than four words [*Complete English Grammar Rules*]:

1. *Sometimes* I had to wait for Edson to decide.

Lesson 12

Replacing omitted words

According to John Hart, he wrote [*Advanced English Grammar*]: The comma is employed to mark the omission of a word (generally a noun or a pronoun or a verb, or both); as, In London we heard fine music; in Paris, better music. Robert is the brighter boy; John, the better student. The black cloth costs a dollar; the blue, two dollars. January, 10th.

The above was extracted from page 166 of the book published in 1898.

- The comma between 'Paris' and 'better' is replacing 'we heard'.
- The comma between 'John' and 'the' is replacing 'is'.
- The comma between 'blue' and 'two' is replacing 'cloth costs'.
- The comma between 'January' and '10th' is replacing 'on the'.

More examples:

1. The soldier fired several bullets, but the policeman, none. [The comma between 'policeman' and 'none' is replacing 'fired'.]

2. I scored five times; Mike, two times. [The comma between 'Mike' and 'two' is replacing 'scored'.]

This comma can be left out. John Eastwood [*Oxford Guide to English Grammar*] wrote the following:

Adrian chose a steak and Lucy spaghetti. [The verb 'chose' is omitted between 'Lucy' and 'spaghetti'.]

This sentence was extracted from page 42 of the *Oxford Guide to English Grammar*.

THE USE OF A SEMICOLON

Like the comma, the semicolon (;) has more than one use:

Lesson 1

List of elements

The use of a semicolon is called for in a list of elements where there is a comma-confusing situation.

Examples:

1. I heard that Sam bought one dog, two cows, one panda and four goats, Peter bought three dogs, one cat, two oxen and one turkey, Mark bought two sheep, one ox and two donkeys and Mavis bought one sheep, one donkey and five hens.

There are confusing commas in the above. It's a bit hard to clarify their roles. This is where semicolons are called for to occupy the positions of the main commas:

2. I heard that Sam bought one dog, two cows, one panda and four goats; Peter bought three dogs, one cat, two oxen and one turkey; Mark bought two sheep, one ox and two donkeys(;) and Mavis bought one sheep, one donkey and five hens.

Now, it's clear. The semicolons have been employed for the main lists, and the commas are for the sub lists.

Lesson 2

Joining two independent sentences

We use a semicolon to join two independent sentences.

Examples:

1. I saw James; I didn't see Peter.
2. Go; don't wait for me.

The above are independent sentences. They're joined with a semicolon or separated with a period (full stop). If you use the period, the sentences will still make sense:

1. I saw James. I didn't see Peter.
2. Go. Don't wait for me.

Note:

If you use a comma instead of a semicolon, your sentence is considered as a sentence with comma splicing:

1. I saw James, I didn't see Peter. [Comma splicing]
2. Go, don't wait for me. [Comma splicing]

Comma splicing simply means joining with a comma. This joint is weak. Don't use the comma in this.

Lesson 3

Separating complements

We use semicolons to separate complements that have something in common. This is common when we're defining a thing, giving complements, one after the other, that are supporting one another in meaning.

Examples:

1. A hunter is one who hunts game for sport or for food; a huntsman or huntswoman. [Dictionary of the Wiktionary]

2. A doctor is a physician; a member of the medical profession; one who is trained and licensed to heal the sick. [Dictionary of the Wiktionary]

In number 1, the complements are 'one who hunts game for sport or for food' and 'a huntsman or huntswoman'. In number 2, the complements are 'a physician', 'a member of the medical profession', and 'one who is trained and licensed to heal the sick'. Each of the complements is supporting the previous one.

THE USE OF A COLON

A colon (:) introduces a phrase or a clause.

Look at the following:

Lesson 1

Introducing a list

The colon introduces a list.

Example:

These are the names of the boys whose surname is Mazira:

- Tinashe
- Nyasha
- Patson
- Tinotenda

Lesson 2

Direct speech

The colon is also used to introduce a direct speech.

Examples:

1. I said: "You've no idea."
2. She spoke to them: "I ain't going to get it."

Lesson 3

Unquoted sentences

Apart from introducing a direct speech, the colon introduces an unquoted sentence—one or more.

Examples:

1. It was a sad moment: the mine collapsed and killed ten workers.

2. It was a sad moment: The mine collapsed and killed ten workers, who had been employed to work underground. They all died on the spot.

Lesson 4

Ratios

The colon is also used in arithmetic for ratios.

Examples:

1. (2:10)

2. (500:10,000)

THE USE OF DASHES

There are only two types of dashes we want to talk about—an *en dash* and an *em dash*.

En dash

The en dash (–) is shorter than the em dash (—). The en dash is usually used to express ranges.

Examples:

1. 5–20 [This means the numbers range from 5 to 20.]
2. 100–500km [This means the kilometres range from 100 to 500.]

Em dash

The em dash (—) is longer than the en dash. It has several uses.

Jane Straus wrote in her book [*The Blue Book of Grammar and Punctuation* (page 69)]: Em dashes may replace commas, semicolons, colons, and parentheses to indicate added emphasis, an interruption, or an abrupt change of thought.

Lesson 1

Parenthesis or interrupters

We use the em dashes to mark off a word, a phrase or a clause that we can also mark off or separate with commas.

Examples:

1. James—*according to the reports I got from those boys yesterday*—is a soldier.

2. James—*I'm sure*—is a soldier.

3. Edson Mazira—*whose several books are on Amazon*—has released a new one.

In this, no spaces should be left around the em dashes; however, some people leave them, but I don't encourage you to be like them. Others even use en dashes in place of em dashes, but I don't encourage you to do that.

Lesson 2

Break

The em dash indicates a break in a direct speech or thought.

Examples:

> "Do you know Jack?" asked Mark.
> "Yes." John nodded.
> Mark said, "He used a catapult to kill an elephant and a—"
> "Stop!" John stood up. "I'm not here for your lies, Mark."

In this dialogue, the em dash indicates a break. Mark was interrupted by John.

No other punctuation mark is used, after the em dash, to end the interrupted sentence:

> "He used a catapult to kill an elephant and a—."

This is wrong with the period ending the interrupted sentence.

Lesson 3

Replacing the colon

The em dash is also used to replace the colon.

Examples:

1. It was a sad moment: the mine collapsed and killed ten workers.
    It was a sad moment—the mine collapsed and killed ten workers.

2. He had weapons: a knife, a pistol and a baton stick.
    He had weapons—a knife, a pistol and a baton stick.

Lesson 4

Replacing the semicolon

We can use the em dash to replace the semicolon.

Examples:

1. I saw John; I didn't see Peter.
   I saw John—I didn't see Peter.

2. Go; don't wait for me.
   Go—don't wait for me.

Lesson 5

Emphasis

The em dashes also show emphasis on the word, phrase or clause they mark off. It's not always that the word, phrase or clause marked off is parenthetical. Sometimes it's marked off for emphasis.

Examples:

1. His book—*this one with the yellow cover*— is going for ten dollars only.

The em dashes are emphasizing the phrase 'this one with the yellow cover'.

THE USE OF ELLIPSES

The ellipsis (...) is normally represented with three dots. It's used to indicate missing or omitted words.

Examples:

1. She picked up two boxes from the ground and handed them over to their owner.

2. She picked up two boxes...handed them over to their owner. [The ellipsis is representing the omitted or missing words: *from the ground and.*]

Don't use the ellipsis to indicate a break or an interruption:

"Do you know Jack?" asked Mark.
"Yes." John nodded.
Mark said, "He used a catapult to kill an elephant and a..." [**Don't use the ellipsis. Use the em dash.**]
"Stop!" John stood up. "I'm not here for your lies, Mark."

The ellipsis can be used for hesitation, not for interruption.

Examples:

"I've some bad news!" said the messenger.

"What bad news?" Sherry was alarmed.
"Your father…" The messenger scratched his head. "Is there any adult person to whom I can leave the message, girl?"

From the above, the messenger was not interrupted by anyone, but he just hesitated to leave the message to Sherry.

THE USE OF A PERIOD

A period (.) is also known as a full stop.

Lesson 1

Ending complete sentences

The period ends a declarative or an imperative sentence. After the ended sentence, another one starting with an uppercase may begin.

Examples:

1. I bought a house. [Declarative]
2. Follow them. [Imperative]
3. Go. [Imperative]

Never leave any space after the last word in order to place the period (or any other punctuation mark):

1. I bought a house . [It's wrong with the space between 'house' and the period '.'.]
2. Follow them . [Wrong]
3. Go . [Wrong]

Lesson 2

Abbreviations

The period is also used to mark abbreviations.

Examples:

1. Z.R.P. (Zimbabwe Republic Police)
2. R.B.Z. (Reserve Bank of Zimbabwe)

When these marked abbreviations come at the end of a declarative or an imperative sentence, you don't need an extra period to end the sentence:

1. This is the Z.R.P.
2. This is the Z.R.P.. [Wrong with an extra period]

Don't put the period before the abbreviation:

1. Mazira .E   [Wrong]
2. Mazira E.   [Correct]

Lesson 3

Phrases

Sometimes, the period ends phrases or single words, some of whose words have been omitted.

Examples:

> *Hulk. He was a huge man. His muscles were like protruding roots of a baobab tree. His head...*
>
> *"What's that?" Pause. "You hear that?"*
>
> *"Yes," the other man whispered, "that must be Hulk walking."*

The period after Hulk does not mean Hulk is a complete sentence. Hulk is just a single word, a noun: Hulk was a huge man.

In the second paragraph, we have 'pause'. After it, there's a period. Is 'pause' a complete sentence? No. It's a single word, a noun, whose other words have been omitted:

> *"What's that?" There was a pause. "You hear that?"*

Periods and semicolons are sometimes used interchangeably:

1. Don't give them money. Instead, teach them to work for it.
   Don't give them money; instead, teach them to work for it.

2. They beat him severely. As a result, he died.
   They beat him severely; as a result, he died.

In the above, the periods have been replaced with the semicolons.

If we use commas to replace these periods, we get sentences with comma splicing:

3. Don't give them money. Instead, teach them to work for it.
   Don't give them money, instead, teach them to work for it.

4. They beat him severely. As a result, he died.

   They beat him severely, as a result, he died.

THE USE OF A QUESTION MARK

A question mark (?) ends an interrogative sentence.

Examples:

1. Do you know Jack?
2. You hear that?
3. Who?
4. Where?
5. You're his brother?
6. She is your sister, isn't she?

Never use a period before or after a question mark to end a sentence:

1. Was it his right.? [Wrong]
2. Was it his right?. [Wrong]

THE USE OF AN EXCLAMATION MARK

An exclamation mark (!) ends a word, phrase or clause expressing excitement, surprise, shock or a shout.

Examples:

1. Wow! I'm happy for you!
2. Ah! This is really shocking!
3. Grr! Get out!
4. Hey! Stop that horse!
5. This is your fault, Mark!
6. Don't touch me!
7. Shut up!
8. Who is that?!

No period (full stop) is required before or after this exclamation mark, but a question mark is okay to form an *interrobang*. This *interrobang* is a combination of a question mark and an exclamation mark—it's originally woven into a single symbol.

THE USE OF BRACKETS

Brackets exist in more than one type: square brackets '[ ]', curly brackets '{ }' and parenthesis brackets '( )'.

At this moment, we are going to look at the parenthesis brackets only.

Lesson 1

Parenthesis

Parenthesis brackets '( )' are used to enclose parenthetical information, the information that's not necessary. These brackets work like the commas and the dashes enclosing non-restrictive relative clauses and non-restrictive appositive nouns.

Examples:

1. James (according to the reports I got from those boys yesterday) is a soldier.
2. Edson Mazira (one of the Zimbabwean authors) is with us tonight.
3. She bought two dresses (a blue dress and a yellow one).

Everything in the brackets is parenthetical and can be removed together with the brackets. When removing them, the essential information is left grammatically correct and making sense.

Look at this:

1. James (according to the reports I got from those boys yesterday) is a soldier. [With parenthesis]
   James is a soldier. [With no parenthesis]

2. Edson Mazira (one of the Zimbabwean authors) is with us tonight. [With parenthesis]
   Edson Mazira is with us tonight. [With no parenthesis]

3. Mavis bought two dresses (a blue dress and a yellow one). [With parenthesis]
   Mavis bought two dresses. [With no parenthesis]

Lesson 2

Wrong placement of periods

Never misplace a period or any other punctuation mark around the brackets:

1. Mavis bought two dresses (a blue dress and a yellow one.)
2. An expert never blows its own trumpet. [This is a proverb].

How do we prove that the above placement of periods is wrong? We do this: We remove the brackets and everything inside them. We spare everything outside the brackets and see if it makes sense.

Let's try this:

1. Mavis bought two dresses (a blue dress and a yellow one.)
   Mavis bought two dresses

Here, after removing the brackets and everything inside them, we're left with a sentence without a period. This makes us understand that the period was supposed to be outside the brackets so that it wouldn't be removed.

Write it this way:

1. Mavis bought two dresses (a blue dress and a yellow one).
   Mavis bought two dresses.

Now, let's look at number 2:

2. An expert never blows its own trumpet. [This is a proverb].
   An expert never blows its own trumpet..

Here, after removing the brackets and everything within them, we're left with a sentence ending with two periods, which is wrong. This makes us understand that the second period was supposed to be within the brackets so that it could be removed together with the brackets.

Write it this way:

2. An expert never blows its own trumpet.
[This is a proverb.]
An expert never blows its own trumpet.

You need to be careful about where to place the periods around the brackets. If the period is only for the parenthesis, let it be within the brackets, but if it's also for the information outside the brackets, let it be outside the brackets as well.

THE USE OF QUOTATION MARKS

Quotation marks are also known as inverted commas, quotes or quotations. They exist in two main types: double quotation marks (" ") and single quotation marks (' '). In each case, we have opening marks (' or ") and closing marks (' or ").

The quotation marks are used to quote a direct speech or a peculiar (outstanding) word, phrase or clause.

Examples:

1. "Do you know Jack?" asked Mark.
   'Do you know Jack?' asked Mark.

2. "Yes." John nodded.
   'Yes.' John nodded.

3. That dog was his "homeboy".
   That dog was his 'homeboy'.

The use of double or single quotes depends on your choice or style.

Lesson 1

Direct speech

In a direct speech, a comma, a period, an exclamation mark or a question mark is always placed on the left side of the nearest inverted comma(s).

Look at this:

1. "Do you know Jack**?**" [The question mark is on the left side of the closing inverted commas.]
2. "Yes**.**" John nodded. [The period is on the left side of the closing inverted commas.]
3. "Watch out**!**" [The exclamation mark is on the left side of the closing inverted commas.]
4. Mavis said**,** "I bought two dresses." [The comma is on the left side of the opening inverted commas.]
5. "I bought two dresses**,**" Mavis said. [The comma is on the left side of the closing inverted commas.]

Lesson 2

Switching to another paragraph within the same quotes

When a direct speech has more than one paragraph, the first paragraph—after being given the opening inverted commas—is not given the closing inverted commas when it's being followed by another paragraph, which is the second paragraph. This second paragraph is only given the opening inverted commas when it's being followed by the third paragraph. The third paragraph—if it's the last one—is then given both the opening and the closing inverted commas. But if it's not the last one, it's not given the closing inverted commas.

Example:

The teacher said, "Punctuation marks are very important. You need to study them. They clarify your writing.

"Everyone who writes in English needs to know them. You can't say they're only for the primary school pupils, nor can you say they're only for the secondary school students.

"Doctors and professors need them, too."

Note that the first paragraph and the second paragraph have no closing inverted commas. This is because it's one person, the teacher, speaking continuously. The closing inverted commas are only given to the last paragraph. Giving them (the closing inverted commas) to every paragraph means different people are speaking, not one person.

Look at this:

The teacher said, "Punctuation marks are very important. You need to study them. They clarify your writing."

"Everyone who writes in English needs to know them. You can't say they're only for the primary school pupils, nor can you say they're only for the secondary school students."

"Doctors and professors need them, too."

In the above, it means someone else is talking with the teacher. The effect has been caused by the closing inverted commas in the first paragraph and the second paragraph. Do you get this?

Lesson 3

Peculiar (outstanding) words, phrases or clauses

The issue of a peculiar word, phrase or clause is different from that of the direct speech. In this, a comma, a period, an exclamation mark or a question mark is placed on the right side of the last quotes.

Examples:

1. That dog was her "homeboy". [The period is on the right side of the last quotes.]
2. Can we call a dog "homeboy"? [The question mark is on the right side of the last quotes.]

Lesson 4

Quotes within other quotes

When you want to quote a word, a phrase or a clause already within quotations, you use other quotes different from those used already.

Examples:

1. Mavis said, "This dog is my 'homeboy.'"
2. Mavis said, 'This dog is my "homeboy."'

When you use double quotes outside, use single quotes inside. When you use single quotes outside, use double quotes inside.

THE USE OF AN APOSTROPHE

An apostrophe (') has a shape similar to that of a closing inverted comma ('), but they're not the same.

The apostrophe has more than one use.

Lesson 1

Possession

We use the apostrophe to form possessive nouns.

Examples:

1. Edson+'+s=Edson's
2. James+'=James' (James's)

Lesson 2

Missing letters

The apostrophe is used to replace missing letters in contracted words.

Examples:

1. Do not = don't
2. Has not = hasn't
3. Are not = aren't
4. You are = you're
5. You would = you'd
6. I will = I'll

EXERCISES

Exercise 1

Insert commas in the following sentences:

1) If I see them I'll tell them.
2) If I'd known it I'd have stopped them.
3) Whenever she thought of going her brother discouraged her.
4) If I ask you a simple question will you answer me?
5) When the game is over everyone will go home.

Exercise 2

Insert commas to mark off non-restrictive relative clauses and non-restrictive appositive nouns or noun phrases from the main clauses:

1) Tinashe Mazira whom we talked to yesterday knows how to fix this.
2) Mr Mazira our teacher of English language wrote a book titled *Punctuation Manual.*
3) Do you remember Gringo the comedian?
4) This is Jacob Banda whom I've been talking about since last year.
5) I know him. He's Jacob Banda the detective.

Exercise 3

Insert commas to mark off nouns of address:

1) I didn't know Mark was your friend John.
2) See you tomorrow Patson.
3) Tinotenda and Patson do you use one surname?
4) Yes Mrs Moyo we're brothers.
5) Class stand up and greet our new friends.

Exercise 4

Remove unnecessary commas from the following sentences:

1) Standing up, and exercising, could help you, stay fit, Jack.
2) Today, is a good day, for us, isn't it?
3) I'll tell, them, if I, see them.
4) My dog, and his cat, are not, friends.
5) My friends, and I'll visit, the orphanage.

Exercise 5

Use commas to separate the interjections or the absolute phrases from the main clauses:

1) Hi I'm Dennis.
2) The old man a big hat on his grey-haired head walked down the road.
3) The sun rising in the East a grey jacket on his shoulder Mr Masiye walked to the bus stop.
4) Umm I've no idea.
5) She narrated her story her hands folded on the table.

Exercise 6

Use coordinating conjunctions of your own choice to join the following independent sentences:

1) Nyasha travelled to Bindura to see his friend. He did not find him.
2) The hunter fired several bullets at the animals. They all ran away.
3) The forest was too dense. It wasn't easy for us to locate the point.
4) He chose to accept my advice. He's my advisor.
5) The bull is too violent. I can't herd it alone.

Exercise 7

Construct three sentences with the serial / Oxford comma and two sentences without the serial / Oxford comma.

Exercise 8

Insert the missing commas:

1) Dande area I am sure was a beautiful place with splendid forests.
2) I talked with Edson Mazira who wrote *Chickens Come Home to Roost*, and Peter Goredema, who wrote a certain book whose title I can't remember.

3) According to the reports I got from those boys, who associate with him James is a soldier.
4) That man if I'm not mistaken is the one I asked about Gringo the comedian.
5) The president of our company, Dr Simba has authorised us to use our new company vehicles.

Exercise 9

Correct the following sentences:

1) Yesterday, was not meant for me, but today, is mine.
2) Driving at night, is not that safe, and must be done with caution.
3) I started, noticing some changes, on her body.
4) I'm a teacher not a soldier.
5) My sister, and I are not coming Mr Dube.

Exercise 10

Insert semicolons and commas in the following list of elements:

Patson studied Mathematics Commerce and Accounts Nyasha studied Physics Biology and Chemistry and Tinashe studied English History and Shona.

Exercise 11

Correct the following run-on sentences:

1) I talked with Mary she's fine.
2) Stop them don't let them get away.
3) Everyone was present that's the first thing I observed.
4) I saw Peter I didn't see James.
5) This one is for me that one is for you.

Exercise 12

Insert em dashes:

1) The hare and the baboon I'm sure you agree with me were personified in many folktales.
2) James I'm sure is a soldier.
3) People according to Charles Darwin developed from apes.
4) Edson Mazira whose dynamic books are on Amazon released a new one.
5) He carried dangerous weapons a gun and a machete.

Exercise 13

Solve some punctuation issues with the following:

1) _____is correct.
   A. ZA.CC   B. Z.A.C.C
   C. Z.A.C.C.   D. Z.ACC.
2) _____is correct.
   A. Mazira. E   B. Mazira. E..

C. Mazira E.   D. Mazira..E.
3) _____is wrong.
   A. 'Where?"   B. "Who?"
   C. 'Yes.'   D. 'You hear that?'
4) _____is wrong.
   A. I'm happy. [This is A].
   B. I'm happy. [This is B.]
   C. I'm happy.
   D. I am happy.
5) _____is correct.
   A. "I realised" she said "I was alone."
   B. "I realised," she said "I was alone."
   C. "I realised," she said, "I was alone.'
   D. "I realised," she said, "I was alone."

Exercise 14

Create possessive nouns from these names, and use them in your own sentences:

1) Charles
2) Peter
3) Mr Browns
4) Mrs Mazira
5) Jack

ANSWERS

Exercise 1

1) If I see them, I'll tell them.
2) If I'd known it, I'd have stopped them.
3) Whenever she thought of going, her brother discouraged her.
4) If I ask you a simple question, will you answer me?
5) When the game is over, everyone will go home.

Exercise 2

1) Tinashe Mazira, whom we talked to yesterday, knows how to fix this.
2) Mr Mazira, our teacher of English language, wrote a book titled *Punctuation Manual*.
3) Do you remember Gringo, the comedian?
4) This is Jacob Banda, whom I've been talking about since last year.
5) I know him. He's Jacob Banda, the detective.

Exercise 3

1) I didn't know Mark was your friend, John.
2) See you tomorrow, Patson.
3) Tinotenda and Patson, do you use one surname?
4) Yes, Mrs Moyo, we're brothers.

5) Class, stand up and greet our new friends.

Exercise 4

1) Standing up and exercising could help you stay fit, Jack.
2) Today is a good day for us, isn't it?
3) I'll tell them if I see them.
4) My dog and his cat are not friends.
5) My friends and I'll visit the orphanage.

Exercise 5

1) Hi, I'm Dennis.
2) The old man, a big hat on his grey-haired head, walked down the road.
3) The sun rising in the East, a grey jacket on his shoulder, Mr Masiye walked to the bus stop.
4) Umm, I've no idea.
5) She narrated her story, her hands folded on the table.

Exercise 6

1) Nyasha travelled to Bindura to see his friend, but he did not find him.
2) The hunter fired several bullets at the animals, and they all ran away.
3) The forest was too dense, so it wasn't easy for us to locate the point.
4) He chose to accept my advice, yet he's my advisor.

5) The bull is too violent, so I can't herd it alone.

Exercise 7

Examples:

1) I bought two shirts, one pair of shoes, and two pairs of socks. [With the serial / Oxford comma]
2) I bought two shirts, one pair of shoes and two pairs of socks. [Without the serial / Oxford comma]

Exercise 8

1) Dande area, I am sure, was a beautiful place with splendid forests.
2) I talked with Edson Mazira, who wrote *Chickens Come Home to Roost*, and Peter Goredema, who wrote a certain book whose title I can't remember.
3) According to the reports I got from those boys, who associate with him, James is a soldier.
4) That man, if I'm not mistaken, is the one I asked about Gringo, the comedian.
5) The president of our company, Dr Simba, has authorised us to use our new company vehicles.

Exercise 9

1) Yesterday was not meant for me, but today is mine.
2) Driving at night is not that safe and must be done with caution.
3) I started noticing some changes on her body.
4) I'm a teacher, not a soldier.
5) My sister and I are not coming, Mr Dube.

Exercise 10

Patson studied Mathematics, Commerce and Accounts; Nyasha studied Physics, Biology and Chemistry and Tinashe studied English, History and Shona.

Note that it's also correct if you've used the serial / Oxford comma.

Exercise 11

1) I talked with Mary; she's fine.
2) Stop them. Don't let them get away.
3) Everyone was present; that's the first thing I observed.
4) I saw Peter; I didn't see James.
5) This one is for me; that one is for you.

Exercise 12

1) The hare and the baboon—I'm sure you agree with me—were personified in many folktales.
2) James—I'm sure—is a soldier.

3) People—according to Charles Darwin—developed from apes.
4) Edson Mazira—whose dynamic books are on Amazon—released a new one.
5) He carried dangerous weapons—a gun and a machete.

Exercise 13

1) (C) Z.A.C.C. is correct.
2) (C) Mazira E. is correct.
3) (A) 'Where?" is wrong.
4) (A) *I'm happy. [This is A].* This is wrong because the period is outside the brackets.
5) (D) "I realised," she said, "I was alone." [This one is correct.]

Exercise 14

Examples:

1) This is *Charles' (Charles's)* car.
2) This is *Peter's* car.
3) This is *Mr Browns'* car.
4) This is *Mrs Mazira's* car.
5) This is *Jack's* car.

CITATION

1. Herring, P. (2016). *Complete English Grammar Rules*. Dublin, Ireland: Farlex International Ltd.
2. Straus, J. (2008). *The Blue Book of Grammar and Punctuation [Tenth Edition]*. San Francisco: Jossey-Bass.
3. Eastwood, J. (1994). *Oxford Guide to English Grammar*. New York: Oxford University Press.

INDEX

www.ingramcontent.com/pod-product-compliance
Lightning Source LLC
Chambersburg PA
CBHW060616030426

42337CB00018B/3071